Lingo Dingo
and the
Greek chef

Written by Mark Pallis
Illustrated by James Cottell

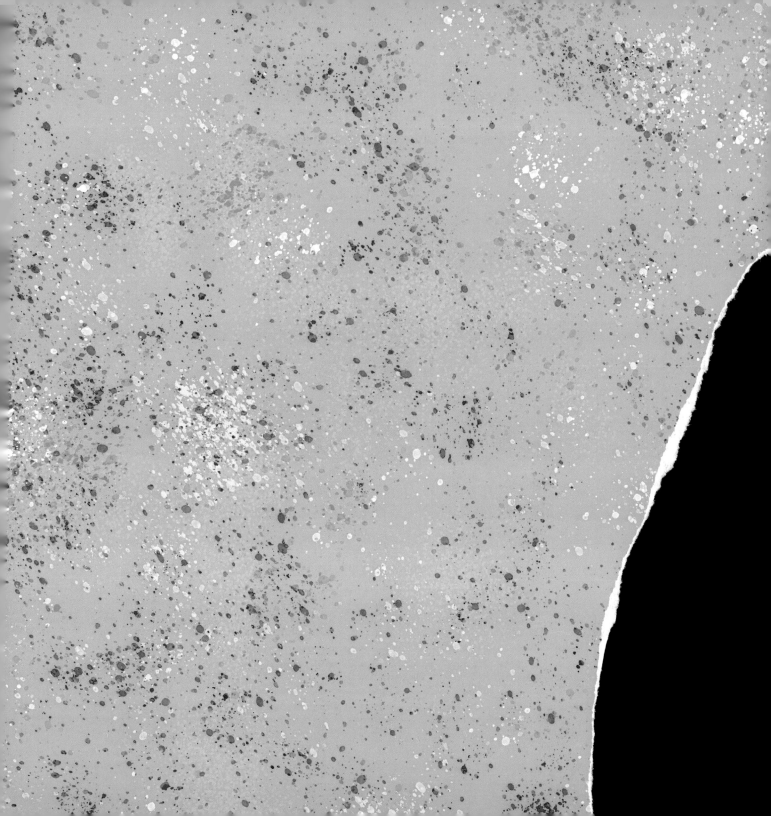

For my awesome sons Oscar and Felix - MP

For Leo and Juniper - JC

LINGO DINGO AND THE GREEK CHEF

Story edited by Natascha Biebow, Blue Elephant Storyshaping
First Printing, 2022
ISBN: 978-1-915337-09-2
NeuWestendPress.com

Lingo Dingo
and the
Greek chef

Written by Mark Pallis

Illustrated by James Cottell

NEU WESTEND
— PRESS —

This is Lingo. She's a Dingo and she loves helping.
Anyone. Anytime. Anyhow.

Lingo often helps her stylish neighbour Gunther, who lives by himself next door. She does a few jobs and has a nice chat. It makes Gunter feel good and it makes Lingo feel good too.

One day, Lingo arranged a special birthday party for Gunther. She even ordered a cake from a famous Greek chef.

There was a knock at the door, "It must be the cake!" said Lingo.

But it was a monkey.

Geia sas. To ónomá mou eínai Sef Nóno
"Γεια σας. Το όνομά μου είναι Σεφ Νόνο.
Écho éna próvlima
Έχω ένα πρόβλημα," he said.

Oh no. I can't speak Greek yet, thought
Lingo. *Maybe 'Γεια σας' is like 'Hello'.*

Γεια σας = Hello; **Το όνομά μου είναι** = My name is;
Έχω ένα πρόβλημα = I have a problem.

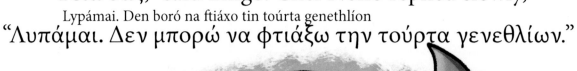

"Γεια σας," said Lingo. Chef Nono replied slowly,
Lypámai. Den boró na ftiáxo tin toúrta genethlíon
"Λυπάμαι. Δεν μπορώ να φτιάξω την τούρτα γενεθλίων."

"I don't understand," said Lingo. "But let me guess. You want..."

Λυπάμαι = I am sorry; **τούρτα γενεθλίων** = birthday cake
Δεν μπορώ να φτιάξω την τούρτα γενεθλίων = I cannot make the birthday cake

Ένα καροτσάκι = a trolley; Ένα αγγουράκι τουρσί = a pickled cucumber / gherkin;
Μπαλόνια = balloons; Όχι = no

O foúrnos mou eínai chalasménos
"Ο φούρνος μου είναι χαλασμένος," explained Chef.
Boró na chrisimopoiíso to foúrno sou
"Μπορώ να χρησιμοποιήσω το φούρνο σου;"

Chef's oven must be broken thought Lingo. "I know!
Let's bake the cake together," she said.

Ο φούρνος μου είναι χαλασμένος = my oven is broken; χαλάσει = broken down;
Μπορώ να χρησιμοποιήσω το φούρνο σου; = can I use your oven?

Chef tapped his wrist. "Τι ώρα είναι? Εννιά? Δέκα ακριβώς?" he asked.

Lingo pointed at her watch.

"Έντεκα! Πάμε! Γρήγορα!"

They only had one hour until the party.

Τι ώρα είναι? = what time is it?; **Εννιά ακριβώς** = nine o'clock; **Δέκα ακριβώς** = ten o'clock; **Έντεκα** = eleven; **Πάμε** = let's go; **Γρήγορα** = quick

Chef Nono and Lingo whizzed around the kitchen:

Μία ποδιά = an apron; για σένα = for you; Ένα σύρμα = a whisk
Ένα μπολ = a mixing bowl

Dóse mou to voútyro, ti záchari,
"Δώσε μου το βούτυρο, τη ζάχαρη,
ta avgá kai to alévri parakaló
τα αυγά και το αλεύρι παρακαλώ," said Chef.

Lingo wasn't sure what those words meant, so she just grabbed fish, coffee and onions instead.

Psária, kafés kai kremmýdia
"Ψάρια, καφές και κρεμμύδια.
Aidía
Αηδία!" laughed Chef.

Δώσε μου = pass me; **βούτυρο** = butter; **ζάχαρη** = sugar; **αυγά** = eggs; **και** = and;
αλεύρι = flour; **παρακαλώ** = please; **Ψάρια** = fish; **καφές** = coffee; **κρεμμύδια** = onions; **Αηδία** = disgusting

Chef plopped butter, sugar, eggs and flour into a bowl. "So that's
what 'βούτυρο, ζάχαρη, αυγά, αλεύρι' means!" laughed Lingo.

voútyro, záchari, avgá, alévri

Egó anakatévo, esý anakatéveis, emeís anakatévoume
"Εγώ ανακατεύω, εσύ ανακατεύεις, εμείς ανακατεύουμε,"

said Chef and together they began to mix the cake.

Εγώ ανακατεύω = I mix; **εσύ ανακατεύεις** = you mix; **εμείς ανακατεύουμε** = we mix

Kai sto télos béjkin páounter. Dýo koutaliés

"Και στο τέλος μπέικιν πάουντερ. Δύο κουταλιές," said Chef.

Lingo guessed 'μπέικιν πάουντερ' meant baking powder, but how much?

Before she could ask, Chef hurried away, saying,

Me synchoreíte, prépei na káno pipí

"Με συγχωρείτε, πρέπει να κάνω πιπί."

Lingo laughed, "I can guess what 'πιπί' means!"

Και = and; **στο τέλος** = finally; **μπέικιν πάουντερ** = baking powder; **Δύο** = two;
κουταλιές = spoonfulls; **Με συγχωρείτε** = excuse me; **πρέπει να κάνω πιπί** = I need to do a wee wee

I wonder if this is too much? thought Lingo as she added ten spoonfulls of 'μπέικιν πάουντερ' to the mix.

She carefully put everything into the oven and before long, a sweet cakey smell filled the kitchen.

μπέικιν πάουντερ = baking powder

"Τι συνέβη? Είναι τεράστιο!" said Chef.

Lingo realised she had added too much baking powder.

"Sorry," she said sheepishly.

Τι συνέβη = what happened
Είναι τεράστιο = it is huge

They somehow got the cake out of the oven but ...

it was so big ...

... they couldn't hold it. "Disaster!" cried Lingo. "Καταστροφή!" wailed Chef.

Katastrofí

Καταστροφή = disaster

"I know what will make you feel better," said Lingo, kindly. 'Eat this ᾽αγγουράκι τουρσί'

angouráki toursí

Aidía. Misó to toursí
"Αηδία. Μισώ το τουρσί," said Chef.

They were running out of time.

αγγουράκι τουρσί = gherkin; Αηδία = disgusting; Μισώ = I hate

"I've got it! Gunther loves hats, so let's turn the cakey mess into a hat cake! " said Lingo.

First she shaped the cake, then she filled balloons with icing.

Next came the best part: POP! POP! POP!

It was a messy job but in the end, the cake looked fantastic.

Kókkino, portokalí, kítrino, prásino, ble. Téleio

"Κόκκινο, πορτοκαλί, κίτρινο, πράσινο, μπλε. Τέλειο!"said Chef.

Κόκκινο = red; **πορτοκαλί** = orange; **κίτρινο** = yellow;
πράσινο = green; **μπλε** = blue; **Τέλειο** = perfect

There was a knock at the door.

I pórta
"Η πόρτα!" said Chef.

It was Gunther, and he was wearing his special hat!

"Thank you. This makes me feel so special," said Gunther.
"You are special," replied Lingo.

Η πόρτα = the door

Gunter was thrilled with his cake.
Chef's deep voice sang "Να ζήσεις Γκούντερ
Na zíseis Nkoúnter
kai chrónia pollá
και χρόνια πολλά..."

Να ζήσεις Γκούντερ και χρόνια πολλά = May you live Gunther, and many years / Happy birthday

Fýsa
"Φύσα!" said Chef.

Gunther blew out all the candles in one puff and everyone tucked in.

Φύσα = blow

Egó tróo, esý tros, aftós tróei, aftí tróei, aftoí tróne

"Εγώ τρώω, εσύ τρως, αυτός τρώει, αυτή τρώει, αυτοί τρώνε,"

laughed Chef.

Emeís tróme

"Εμείς τρώμε!" added Lingo proudly.

Εγώ τρώω = I eat; εσύ τρως = you eat; αυτός τρώει = he eats;
αυτή τρώει = she eats; αυτοί τρώνε = they eat; Εμείς τρώμε = we eat

The friends watched the sunset. They felt great.

Egó eímai charoúmenos,
"Εγώ είμαι χαρούμενος,

esý eísai charoúmenos
εσύ είσαι χαρούμενος,

Eímaste óloi charoúmenoi
Είμαστε όλοι χαρούμενοι!" cheered Chef.

Εγώ είμαι χαρούμενος = I am happy; **εσύ είσαι χαρούμενος** = you are happy;
Είμαστε όλοι χαρούμενοι = we are all happy

Baking a cake, helping a friend,
learning a new language... what a day!

But now it was time for bed. It was time to dream about
all the fun things that might happen tomorrow.

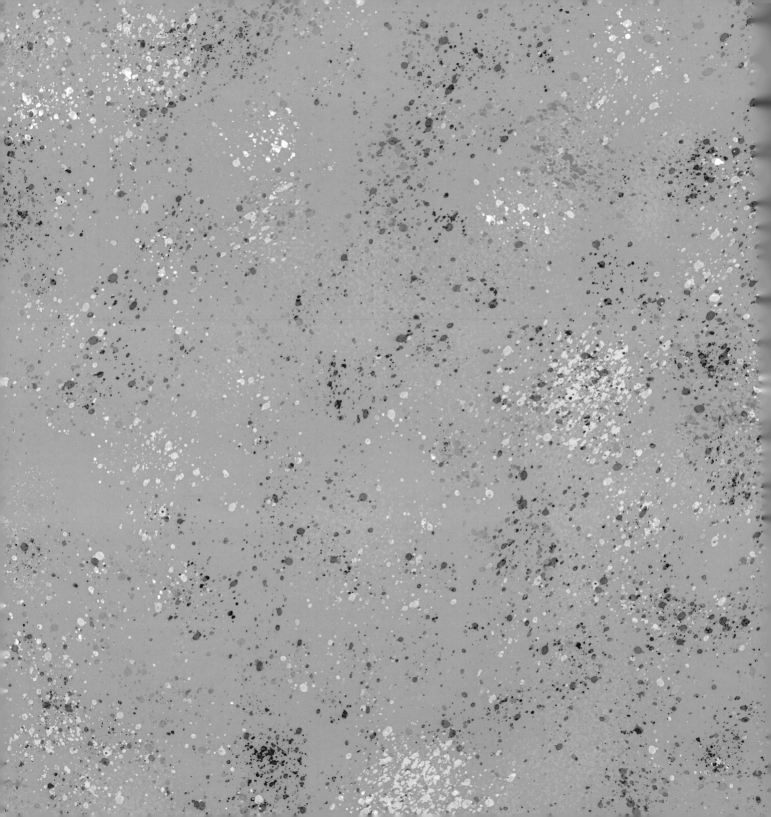

Learning to love languages

An additional language opens a child's mind, broadens their horizons and enriches their emotional life. Research has shown that the time between a child's birth and their sixth or seventh birthday is a "golden period" when they are most receptive to new languages. This is because they have an in-built ability to distinguish the sounds they hear and make sense of them. The Story-powered Language Learning Method taps into these natural abilities.

How the Story-powered language learning Method works

We create an emotionally engaging and funny story for children and adults to enjoy together, just like any other picture book. Studies show that social interaction, like enjoying a book together, is critical in language learning.

Through the story, we introduce a relatable character who speaks only in the new language. This helps build empathy and a positive attitude towards people who speak different languages. These are both important aspects in laying the foundations for lasting language acquisition in a child's life.

As the story progresses, the child naturally works with the characters to discover the meanings of a wide range of fun new words. Strategic use of humour ensures that this subconscious learning is rewarded with laughter; the child feels good and the first seeds of a lifelong love of languages are sown.

For more information and free learning resources visit www.neuwestendpress.com

You can learn more words and phrases with these hilarious, heartwarming stories from NEU WESTEND — PRESS —

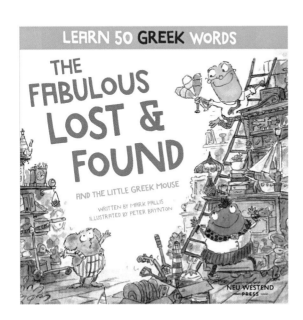

LEARN 50 **GREEK** WORDS

THE FABULOUS LOST & FOUND

AND THE LITTLE GREEK MOUSE

WRITTEN BY MARK PALLIS
ILLUSTRATED BY PETER BAYNTON

NEU WESTEND
PRESS

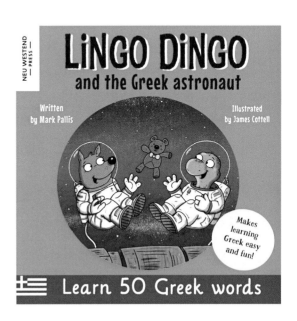

NEU WESTEND — PRESS —

LINGO DINGO
and the Greek astronaut

Written by Mark Pallis

Illustrated by James Cottell

Makes learning Greek easy and fun!

Learn 50 Greek words

CERTIFICATE

Dear _____

Congratulations

You are learning a new language.

You are a **star!**

With my best wishes

Lingo

NEU WESTEND
PRESS

> "I want people to be so busy laughing, they don't realise they're learning!"
>
> Mark Pallis

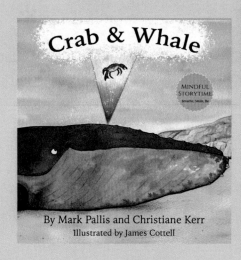

Crab and Whale is the bestselling story of how a little Crab helps a big Whale. It's carefully designed to help even the most energetic children find a moment of calm and focus. It also includes a special mindful breathing exercise and affirmation for children.

Featured as one of Mindful.org's 'Seven Mindful Children's books'

Do you call them hugs or cuddles?

In this funny, heartwarming story, you will laugh out loud as two loveable gibbons try to figure out if a hug is better than a cuddle and, in the process, learn how to get along.

A perfect story for anyone who loves a hug (or a cuddle!)

www.markpallis.com